HYDROPONICS:

THE BEGINNER'S GUIDE TO CHOOSE YOUR
BEST SUSTAINABLE GARDENING SYSTEM
AND GROW ORGANIC VEGETABLES AT
HOME WITHOUT SOIL.

Max Gordon

TABLE OF CONTENTS

Introduction

The development of hydroponics has not only been a response to the current food and resource problems. It is a solution for the future too. Experts say that by 2050, about 80% of all the food produced will be consumed in the cities, which makes it important for the cities to become producers of food. Currently, most cities are the good 'black holes' because all they do is suck in much of it, and at the same time, the cities are the biggest food wasters.

It is easy to see the wastefulness and excessive nature of normal food production in comparison to hydroponics. To supply food to the urban areas, producers need to produce it in large amounts and to transport it there, sometimes, across vast distances, before it is introduced into the market. From the initial step of production, harvesting, packaging, and shipping, the food takes up large amounts of resources that could be saved and re-used elsewhere. People are involved, pollution-causing fuels, buildings, and other resources, and this is wasteful, in comparison to what hydroponics entails.

As the world's population is getting close to 7.5 billion and the demand for more food increasing just as fast, with emphasis on resource-intensive foods, it is clear that farming needs to be done even in the cities, and even so, more productively.

The supplements utilized in hydroponic frameworks can emerge out of a variety of various sources, including (yet not restricted to) from fish stool, duck compost, or bought substance manures.

Plants regularly developed hydroponically include tomatoes, peppers, cucumbers, lettuces.

Chapter 1

What Is Hydroponics Gardening?

If we break down the word 'hydroponics,' there are two parts – 'hydro' and 'ponics.' Both these words have a meaning where 'hydro' means water, and 'ponics,' which is derived from the word 'ponos' means labor. One of the famous examples of hydroponics culture is in the Hanging Gardens of Babylon. If you think that hydroponics is a relatively new concept, then you are wrong because the mention of it has been found even in the hieroglyphic records of the Egyptians. Did you know that it was even used during World War II? Yes, the non-arable islands had troops stationed on them and in order to sustain life, hydroponic systems were installed to come up with fresh produce.

So, what is hydroponics? Well, it is a scientific method by which you can grow plants in a medium different from the soil. The media is rich in nutrients and water-based. The media also has to be inert, and some of the common types of media used are peat moss, perlite, vermiculite, clay pellets, and so on.

The major question that everyone has is whether a hydroponics system is better than soil or not. Well, I would say that it is quite debatable because both types have their own advantages and disadvantages. Moreover, you should also know that you cannot grow every type of plant with the help of the hydroponic system. But you are also going to be surprised by how many important plants can be grown by this method, the best exampled being carrots and potatoes.

Debunking Myths About Hydroponics

Before we move on to the benefits of hydroponics, let me debunk some common myths about this method. These misconceptions have to be clarified in the beginning; otherwise, you will not be able to embrace this method fully and remain skeptical throughout the book.

It Is Not a Simple Process

If we are talking about the bygone era, then this statement could have been deemed to be true, but as of now, hydroponics is a really easy method of growing plants. Some people use this statement without even knowing what hydroponics really is. Everything starting from preparing the correct nutrient solution to adjusting the necessary lighting is an easy process and I am going to explain it all to you in this book. The job has become even more uncomplicated because of the fact that nutrient solutions are available in the premixed state and so you do not have to figure out the proportion of nutrients by yourself. So, what you have to do is finally add the required amount of mater to this pre-mixed nutrient.

It Is Rocket Science

If you ask about among your friends or family, most of them will tell you that hydroponics is probably like some kind of scientific experiment. This myth mostly arises from the fact that hydroponics involves the usage of tubes, troughs, gauges, and meters. But it is not rocket science. If you are passionate about growing plants but have some barriers in your path, hydroponics can probably solve them for you. If you are a beginner and too tense to start, then you can even get one of the starting kits from the market so that you do not have to do anything on your own. Everything will be explained in the manual.

Hydroponics Is Meant For Growing Plants Indoors Only

It is true that hydroponics is about maintaining a controlled environment for growing plants, but it does not restrict the process to indoors only. You can practice it indoors or outdoors as long as you are following all the guidelines. If you read a bit about the commercial hydroponic growers, you will know that they are done outdoors, but yes, inside a greenhouse, so that a controlled environment can be maintained.

Crops Grown In This Method Are Tasteless

Maximum critics of this method will tell you that there is no taste and flavor in the crops that are grown with the help of hydroponics, but this is a completely baseless claim. If both types of crops are placed in front of you, you will not be able to differentiate between them and tell them apart. Moreover, you should be aware of the fact that the taste of nutrients does not depend on the way that you are growing it but on the nutrient that the crop has absorbed. With hydroponics, you are providing the plant with a nutrient-rich solution, and as long as you are doing that, your crops should be fine. If you talk about reality, then you will know that the crops grown by the method of hydroponics actually have more flavor and nutritional value when compared with the crops grown in the traditional method.

The Process Is Expensive

If we are talking about setting up the system, then I would say that it is not inexpensive. But once you have set it up and plants are growing, the benefits are going to cover whatever money you have invested in the system and provide you excellent returns.

Benefits of Hydroponics

Now, let's move on to the topic of all the benefits that you are going to get by implementing this method. There are a lot of advantages, and we are going to discuss them one by one –

Hydroponics Does Not Depend on Weather Conditions

One of the biggest hurdles in the path of growing something is the weather. If the weather does not permit, then you cannot grow what you want. But this problem can be solved by hydroponics. Suppose you have planted some seeds, and then you get the little saplings, but they do not perform just because there was untimely rain. Can you help it? No, but you can definitely grow your plants in a different method that would help you tackle the weather. You do not have to worry about a late frost or early rain because you can completely control the environment in which you are growing your crops in the case of hydroponics. Moreover, hydroponics advises you to grow your plants indoors or if you want to do it outdoors, then do it inside a greenhouse so that there is no issue of weather at all.

You Don't Have to Worry About the Season

Every plant has its own season, and you cannot grow it outside that season because the plant will not thrive as it is not getting optimal or even sub-optimal growing conditions. There are even certain times of the year where growing anything is not possible at all. This is even truer if you live in the Northern United States or in Canada because both of these regions have a very limited growing season. So, when winter comes, you cannot grow most of the crops. Your crops need sufficient time to mature, and if winter is prevalent for the most part of the year, then your crops are not going to get enough time to mature as well.

But when you have constructed a hydroponic system, you will get everything throughout the year, and you can control the light and heat as per your requirement. Just imagine, you have the chance to have that nice and hot tomato soup (that did not come out of a can) when the world outside is fully covered in snow. If you are someone who lives in a place that has a colder climate for the maximum part of the year, hydroponics is definitely going to change your life forever.

The Method Involved Less Use of Water

If you probe into the matter deeply, then you will soon realize that it is quite inefficient to grow your plants in soil in those areas where water is not easily available. If water is scarce, growing plants become expensive but not with a hydroponic system. This is because in the case of a hydroponic system, water is utilized very efficiently, and water is required in quite a less amount. The main reason behind this is the contained nature of the hydroponic system. Water can escape this system only if is evaporated or if it is used up by the plants itself. But if the same plants were grown in soil, a lot of water would have been absorbed in the soil or it would have simply run off.

You Don't Have to Worry About Pests

If you are someone who has had a bad experience with pests, then you know what trouble it can be. Cauliflowers being devoured by caterpillars is a very common problem. But these problems occur when you are planting your crops outside in the soil. In order to eradicate the problem, you will either have to be okay with the fact that half of your crops will be lost to the pests, or you have to engage in companion planting. When you install a hydroponic system, your plants will be grown in a closed environment indoors where everything is controlled. That is why a pest infestation is something of a rare occurrence. Yes, you might get occasional pest problems but if you follow some simple measures, you will be able to spot them early and prevent them from causing too much damage.

Hydroponic Plants Are Free of Diseases

Diseases are another one of the problems that you are going to face if you choose to grow your crops outside. For example, if you are growing tomatoes or potatoes, your crops always tend to catch blight. And there is nothing worse than losing all that you have grown because of a simple disease. Sprays for certain diseases are indeed available in the market, which can prevent them. Still, there are certain diseases for which there is no treatment available. The occurrence of diseases becomes scarce when the plants are being grown indoors in a hydroponic system. This is because you will get the chance to quarantine the new plants even before installing them in the system and practicing proper hygiene will help your crops steer clear of any form of diseases.

There Is No Hassle of Digging

There is a good reason behind more and more people adopting the hydroponic system for growing plants at home. One of these reasons is that the process does not involve the hassle of digging. If you are growing your plants in the soil, digging is a major task and often involves a lot of effort. But since hydroponics does not require any soil, so there is no digging as well.

Fewer Artificial Chemicals Are Used

It is true that people now are steering away from chemicals as far as possible even in traditional gardening. Still, even then, through agents like rain and wind, artificial chemicals have a chance of being introduced in the soil. And then there are some gardeners who always prefer the usage of artificial fertilizers and pesticides. But when you grow the plants hydroponically, you can stay far away from chemicals.

Chapter 2

Types Of Hydroponics System

There are hundreds of methods of hydroponic gardening. However, all these are combinations or variations of six basic types:

1. Water Culture

2. Wicks

3. Nutrient Film Techniques

4. Flood and Drains

5. Drips

6. Aeroponics

The following paragraphs give descriptions of the basic hydroponic systems and details how each of them works.

The Water Culture

The Water Culture System is the purest form of active hydroponics. The plants are commonly grown on a medium made of Styrofoam and they grow directly from the nutrient solution. This system uses an air pump to supply oxygen to the plants' roots.

The Water Culture System is the best choice for growing water-loving plants such as lettuce. However, this system is not suitable for many long term or large plants, and these will not thrive using this system.

It is not expensive to make this type of hydroponic system. You can use an old aquarium or water container. It is the ideal set-up for a classroom. This makes it a popular choice for teachers and students.

The Wick System

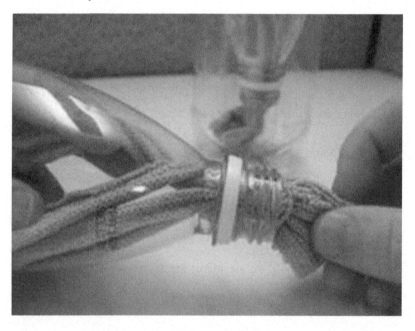

Wicking is the purest form of passive hydroponics. Passive means there are no moving parts in the system. The nutrient solution comes up through the wick from the reservoir and feeds the growing medium through this wick.

The growing mediums used for this system are coconut fiber, pro-mix, vermiculite and perlite. It is an effective system for small plants because large plants tend to draw up the nutrient solution faster than the wicks can supply them.

Nutrient Film Technique

The Nutrient Film Technique or NFT is the most prevalent type of hydroponics. It is probably the cheapest and easiest to create. The benefit of this system is that no soil is used. The roots of the plants are suspended directly in water and the nutrient solution is pumped into the water that covers the roots and drained back into a reservoir.

There is no need for a timer and you do not have to replace the growing medium after every change of crop. The NFT usually makes use of a small plastic basket that has been designed to let the roots dangle into the nutrient solution. The only drawback is that when power outages and pump failures occur, the flow of solution is interrupted and the roots tend to dry out quickly.

The Flood And Drain System

This is known as the "Ebb and Flow." It works by flooding the growing medium or tray with the nutrient solution and draining it back to the reservoir. This action is achieved by a submersible pump, which is connected to a pre-set timer.

The timer will trigger the pump to siphon the nutrient solution onto the tray. After this action, the timer will also shut the pump off so that the solution will ebb back. The gardener will set the timer to turn on several times during the day – the frequency will be dependent on several factors:

- Type of plant
- Size of plant
- Temperature
- Humidity
- Growing medium

The grow tray can be filled with different growing mediums. The most popular choices are rockwool, perlite, gravel, coconut fiber and grow rocks. Most people use individual pots as trays.

The main challenge with the "Ebb and Flow" system is the susceptibility to power outages, pump failures, and timer failures. Some mediums like gravel and grow rocks will not hold the nutrient solution well enough so the roots will dry out quickly when the cycle is interrupted. It is better to use rockwool, coconut fiber, and pro-mix as they retain more water.

Drip System

The Drip System is the most widely used hydroponic system. It is set-up with a timer, a submerged pump, and a grow tray. The timer is set to turn the pump on to allow the nutrient solution to drip off directly onto the plants through a small drip line.

There are two kinds of Drip Systems: Recovery and Non-Recovery. In a Recovery Drip, the surplus nutrient solution that flows down is collected in a reservoir and re-used.

The Recovery Drip System is more efficient and less expensive. Apart from being able to re-use the excess nutrient solution, the system does not need precise control for the watering cycles. The timer needs to be more precise in a Non-Recovery Drip System. Hence, the plants get enough of the nutrient solution and there is minimal runoff.

The Recovery System requires more maintenance in recycling the solution back to the reservoir and the pH and strength of the nutrient solution needs to be preserved. This requires periodic testing and adjusting so that pH and strength levels do not shift. On the other hand, the Non-Recovery System needs less maintenance, as the solution is not re-used.

AEROPONICS

A timer triggers the misting pump, similar to on the other hydroponic systems. The only difference is that there is a shorter cycle for the pump. It is a quite delicate and complicated system. There should be no interruption to misting cycles. Otherwise, the roots will dry out quickly.

Chapter 3

Advantages And Disadvantages Of Hydroponics

Any system of growing produce is going to have advantages and disadvantages. It is a good idea to be aware of what these are before you start your DIY system. We will begin by looking at the advantages.

The Advantages

Grow anywhere

There are large areas of the world that can't be used to grow food, specifically deserts and dry regions. But, providing you can get water to these places, you can set up a hydroponics system and grow crops.

Considering much of the space in a dessert is classified as 'useless,' that is a real bonus! It doesn't even matter what the soil is made of.

Fewer pests

Soil-borne pests often attack plants. Because soil is not an essential part of a hydroponics system, the risk of disease is reduced. It should be noted that it is not eliminated as air-borne pests can still introduce diseases to your hydroponics system.

Greenhouses or indoor growing setups act as a barrier for pests. One of the advantages of a greenhouse is that you can release beneficial insects that eat pests. If you are using a greenhouse, these beneficial insects are contained.

Faster growing time

Plants that are grown in hydroponics will grow more quickly because they have access to all the nutrients and trace elements. They provide more yield and are more pest resistant. In short, hydroponics gives better results than conventional farming methods.

Research shows that lettuce grown hydroponically can yield as much as eighty-eight pounds/ ten feet squared (forty-one kilograms/meter squared) a year. As opposed to just eight and a half pounds/ ten feet squared (three point nine kilograms/meter squared) a year when grown conventionally.

Water usage was ten times lower with hydroponics than soil-grown crops. Harvest was 11 times greater with hydroponics than soil.

These numbers seem to speak for themselves, but you have additional costs when doing hydroponics, which have to be factored in. In this study, they also calculated that the energy cost was 82 times greater in hydroponics than soil. This is very important to know for commercial operations.

Better Control

Hydroponics farming allows you to monitor and adjust the nutrients in the water. This gives you much more control over the growing environment, helping to produce the best possible yield in the shortest possible time.

Water Usage

Research concludes that hydroponics uses ninety percent less water than growing plants conventionally in the field. This is because the water is re-circulated most of the times, water is only lost through evaporation or a water exchange.

The Disadvantages

With the advantages, you will always have disadvantages.

Let's look at them next.

High set-up costs

Hydroponics has higher start-up costs than soil-grown crops. This is because you need several items to start with:

- A water tank

- A pump to re-circulate the water

- A setup for your plants to grow (NFT, DWC)

- A grow medium

- The need to buy nutrients

- Sometimes artificial light sources

Airborne diseases

Although the risk of soil-based diseases is lower, air-borne diseases can happen. Because of the nature of hydroponics, these diseases can quickly spread between plants because they are planted closer to each other.

It is essential to be aware of the main signs of plant disease and react a fast as possible.

Another example of a disease that is not airborne is Pythium (root rot), which can be introduced to a hydroponic system through the water and will result in browning of the roots. Luckily, you can control most of these by proper design of the system, which we will talk about later in the book.

Knowledge

Understanding the principles behind hydroponics is relatively straightforward, although some learning is necessary. However, to properly run the system, you need to understand the different pieces of equipment involved and how to monitor and adjust nutrient levels.

Getting this right is essential to creating a long-lasting system, but it can be a steep learning curve. If you are not having success from the first time, see it as a learning experience and not as a defeat.

Monitoring

If you grow crops using conventional soil-based methods, you'll be able to leave your plants for several days. Nature has a habit of finding a way to help plants grow in almost any situation.

If you've created a hydroponics system, you should check for visible problems and check the nutrient levels quite often.

Having a mechanical failure can have an extremely negative effect on your hydroponics system, potentially killing your plants!

Of course, there are several ways to automate parts of the system, but this should not be your primary concern when you create your first hobby system.

Electricity

Electricity is essential to run the pumps, supply artificial light, heating or cooling, and air movement. All these additions will result in a higher electrical bill, which is an additional cost.

Water and electricity do not generally mix well, making this a safety risk that you need to be aware of.

If anything happens to the electricity supply, your plants can suffer surprisingly quickly. You should have a back-up option to run the pump for a few hours in a commercial system. This can be done with a solar setup or a backup generator.

Chapter 4

Guide And Advice In Choosing The Best Hydroponics System

While there is nobody best developing media for all circumstances, some developing media's work superior to others in various frameworks. With any hydroponic framework, as well as a developing media, the objective is as yet the equivalent. You simply need the roots to be clammy, not wet and immersed. And when the developing media is immersed and saturated, the roots will choke from absence of oxygen. That circumstance can without much of a stretch lead to roots kicking the bucket, and root spoil.

Interesting points about developing media for each sort of hydroponic framework

Dribble frameworks

Dribble frameworks are genuinely simple to control dampness in. For whatever length of time that you plan it. Hence, it has great seepage, and utmost water pooling at the base you ought to have the option to shield your developing media from being excessively saturated. We like to utilize waterway shake at the base to help waste, and shield the developing media from sitting in a pool of water at the base.

NFT frameworks

NFT frameworks utilize a shallow, yet consistent stream of water at the base of a channel where the roots wick up dampness. Most NFT frameworks either utilize little starter 3D shapes or little 1 inch containers, at that point let the roots simply hang down into the streaming water. And when these 3D squares or crates are to near the water supply, and your developing media can end up soaked effectively, that mix can prompt "stem decay" if the developing media around the stem is immersed continuously.

Ebb-Flow (flood and channel) frameworks

Flood and channel frameworks can shift a lot in plan. However, by and large you would need to avoid any developing media that buoys like Perlite and Vermiculite. Each time the framework cycles on for the flooding stage the developing media will wind up weightless, at that point your plants will free the entirety of their help and need to spill. Contingent upon your framework you could bring down the flood level. Hence, drifting is insignificant, as long as the root-ball can even now get a lot of dampness and you don't free a lot of plant support. Plant backing may not be as a lot of a factor if developing vine type plants like tomatos, peas or melons that would be attached to a trellis too.

Additionally with flood and channel frameworks, and relying upon the sort of developing media you pick, you need to ensure you have significant seepage. Hence, the developing media isn't ceaselessly soaked. Develop rocks won't wick up much dampness, however we like utilizing coco chips a great deal since they are reasonable, yet coco chips wick up water And when they are sitting in it. So a layer of stream shake at the base shields it from sitting in the water.

Water culture frameworks

Water culture frameworks don't by and large utilize a lot if any developing media since it is structured so the plants roots are submerged into the supplement arrangement itself. So plants are by and large begun utilizing little starter 3D shapes or little bushels. Starter solid shapes typically are suspended over the water line. In contrast, containers can suspended either only above or just underneath the water line. The developing media you pick and the amount it assimilates dampness will have any kind of effect. You don't need it to end up immersed, you simply need it to be wet at the base, and the top ought to be dry. The roots will become descending into the supplement arrangement.

Presently you might think about whether it's so awful if the developing media winds up soaked, for what reason the roots won't become suffocated if their submerged all the time in a water culture framework. First not all plants do well in water culture frameworks. Second and most significant, a water culture framework utilizes a vacuum apparatus to create a great deal of air pockets to the roots submerged. The plants get oxygen from these air bubbles legitimately, just as the air pockets increment the broke down oxygen levels in the water itself.

Aeroponic frameworks

Aeroponic frameworks ordinarily don't utilize a lot of developing media by any stretch of the imagination. Aeroponic frameworks are intended to permit the roots linger palpably while getting now and again getting moistened with supplement arrangement so the roots don't dry out. Seeds are begun in either little starter shapes little crates, at that point when their massive enough their planed in the aeroponic framework. You'll need to ensure the solid shapes or developing media in the containers don't end up immersed. While practically every one of the roots will hang in air with no way of getting to be choked, wet developing media around the plants steam can prompt "stem decay."

Wick frameworks

Wick frameworks are the least utilized sort of framework, however with no moving parts, engines or siphons, they depend on wicking up dampness into the developing media and to the plants roots through a bit of texture. With wick frameworks you'll need to utilize a developing media that ingests and clutches dampness effectively. You can control the measure of water getting to the plant by utilizing a more significant/more large wick, or multiple.

Rundown of various kinds of developing media for hydroponics

Rockwool

Rockwool is one of the most well-known developing media's utilized in hydroponics. Rockwool is a clean, porous, non-degradable medium that is made basically out of stone and additionally limestone which is too warmed and liquefied, at that point spun into a little strings like cotton treats. The rock wool is then shaped into squares, sheets, blocks, sections, or running. Rockwool sucks up water expertly so you'll need to be mindful so as not to give it a chance to end up immersed, or it could choke out your plants roots, just as lead to stem decay and root spoil. Rockwool ought to be pH adjusted before use. That is finished by absorbing its pH adjusted water before use.

Develop Rock (Hydrocorn)

Develop shake is a Lightweight Expanded Clay Aggregate (L.E.C.A.), that is a sort of dirt which is super-terminated to make a porous surface. It's overwhelming enough to give secure help to your plants, yet at the same time light weight. Develop rocks are a non-degradable, clean developing medium that holds dampness, has a neutral pH, and will wick up supplement answer for the root frameworks of your plants. Hydrocorn develop media is reusable, it very well may be cleaned, disinfected, at that point reused once more. Although on an enormous scale, cleaning and sanitizing a lot of develop rocks can be very tedious. Develop shake is one of the most prominent developing medium utilized for hydroponics, and pretty much every store selling hydroponics supplies conveys it.

Coco Fiber Coco Chips

In spite of the fact that coco coir is a natural plant material, it separates and disintegrates gradually, so it won't give any supplements to the plants developing in it, making it ideal for hydroponics. Coco coir is likewise pH impartial, holds dampness well overall, yet still takes into account excellent air circulation for the roots. Coco fiber comes in two structures, coco coir (fiber), and coco chips.

The bigger size of the coco chips takes into account more excellent air pockets between particles, therefore permitting far and away superior air circulation for the roots. Likewise if your utilizing containers to develop your plants in, the chips are to enormous to fall through the braces in the bushels. Both the fibre and chips come in compacted blocks, and once absorbed water it extends to around multiple times the original size. Coco fibre tends to shade the water, however that lessens after some time. Also, you can drain out the vast majority of the shading and when you absorb it warm/high temp water a couple of times before use.

Perlite

Perlite is principally made out of minerals that are exposed to extremely high warmth, which at that point extend it like popcorn so it turns out to be light weight, permeable and spongy. Perlite has an unbiased pH, brilliant wicking activity, and is exceptionally permeable. Perlite can by utilized independent from anyone else, or blended with different sorts of developing media's. Anyway on the grounds that perlite is light to the point that it skims, contingent upon how you structured your hydroponic framework, perlite without anyone else may not be the best decision of developing media for flood and channel frameworks.

Perlite is generally utilized in gardening soils, and any nursery should convey sacks of it. Anyway perlite is now and again additionally utilized as an added substance added to bond. You may discover it at a superior cost with the structure supplies, and additionally at spots that sell cement blends and blending supply's. When working with perlite be mindful so as not to get any of the residue in your eyes. Rinse it off to clean out the residue, and wet it down before working with it to shield the residue from going airborne.

Vermiculite

As a developing media, vermiculite is very like perlite aside from that it has a moderately high cation-trade limit, which means it can hold supplements for later use. Additionally like the perlite, vermiculite is exceptionally light and will in general buoy. There are various uses and kinds of vermiculite, so you'll need to be sure what you get is planned for agriculture use. The simplest method to be sure is to get it from a nursery.

Desert garden Cubes

Desert garden Cubes are like Rockwool blocks, and have comparable properties. However, desert garden 3D squares are progressively similar to the unbending green or white botanical froth utilized by backwoods to hold the stems in their blossom shows. Desert garden solid shapes are an open cell material which implies that the cells can ingest water and air. The open cells wick dampness all through the material, and the roots can without much of a stretch develop and extend through the open cell structure. While desert garden 3D shapes are generally utilized as starter 3D squares for hydroponically developed plants, they additionally have packs you can fill your developing compartments with. While desert spring 3D squares are like rock wool, Oasis 3D shapes don't end up waterlogged as effectively as rock wool blocks. Indeed, even so don't give it a chance to remain in steady contact with the water supply, or regardless you'll have water logging issues.

Botanical froth

Botanical froth can be utilized as a developing media in hydroponics also, and is like the desert garden 3D squares, however the cell size is more significant in the flower froth. Contingent upon the sort of hydroponic framework your utilizing, and how you structured it, you may see two or three issues with utilizing flower froth. First it can disintegrate effectively and that can leave particles in your water. Second you'll need to be sure it doesn't get water logged. Flower froth assimilates water effectively, so ensure it isn't in steady contact with the water supply.

Chapter 5

How To Build A Hydroponics Garden

I n this section, let us look at simple steps you can follow to build these different hydroponic systems at home. If you like DIY projects or arts and crafts, you will undoubtedly enjoy building these systems.

DIY Wick System

Step 1: Materials required

The wick system is the most straightforward hydroponic system you can create at home. Here is the list of materials you will require.

- 2-liter plastic or soda bottle: 1

- 24" cotton string or rope: 6 pieces

- Coconut coir: 2/3 cups

- Perlite: 1/3 cup

- Water: 4 cups

- Seeds: of your choice

- Marker: 1

- Craft knife or cutting blade: 1

- Ruler: 1

- Drill or hammer with nail: 1

- Cutting mat: 1

Note: The best grow media for wick hydroponics systems are coconut coir and perlite.

Step 2: Measure and cut

Take the plastic bottle, measure from the bottom, and make a mark at 8 inches on the bottle. Mark it with a permanent marker and ensure that it is even on all the sides. You need to mark two equidistant points on either side of the plastic bottle measuring 8" from the bottom. Take a craft knife or a blade and cut the top off the bottle by following the markings you made. Now, invert the top portion of the bottle and place it in the bottom half. The top portion will be inverted in a conical fashion, while the bottom serves as a reservoir.

Step 3: Drilling

Now, it is time to start drilling the caps to create the wick system. If you have an electric drill, use it, and this step becomes more relaxed. If not, you can always opt for a hammer, craft knife, and a nail. You need to drill a hole in the bottle's cap. Before you drill the hole, mark the size of the hole you want to create. Alternatively, once you have marked the spot, take a nail and hammer it into the cap. Remove the nail and then cut away the plastic, which sticks out to create sufficient space for inserting the wicks.

Step 4: Placing the wicks

According to the thickness of the cotton string you use, you might be required to loop it a couple of times. The string must be at least one-fourth an inch in its thickness so that the moisture can be drawn into the growing media and then absorbed by the roots. Measure about 12 inches of string and then cut it off. Take the cap with holes drilled in it and push this string through the hole. Place it such that the cap acts as the halfway mark on the string. Tie the string into a knot on the underside of the cap so that it stays as close to the cap as possible.

Step 5: Growing medium

It is time to mix the growing media. To do this, mix coco coir, along with perlite. If you are using any other growing media, merely place them in the top half of the bottle. While doing this, ensure that you hold onto the wick so that it stays fixed in the bottle without getting disturbed. Once you have filled the top part of the bottle with growing media, remove it from the bottom half and place it aside. Now, combine the nutrient mix with about four cups of water. Place the top half of the bottle into the bottom portion and pour this mixture into this setup.

Step 6: Plant seeds

Start planting seeds at the required depth, and that's about it. If you are using artificial grow lights, then set them up near the hydroponic system and wait for the seeds to germinate. Alternatively, you can also place them in the sunlight.

The best plants for a wick system include rosemary, basil, lettuce, chicory, oregano, thyme, and comfrey.

DIY Nutrient Film Technique

Step 1: Basic idea

The hydroponic system based on the Nutrient Film Technique (NFP) requires a reservoir from which water will be drawn and returned to simultaneously. This specific design features two gullies that allow water to be quickly cycled through the system. When coupled with a water pump, the system uses the pull of gravity for assisting the flow of water. The end of the PVC in this system is an inch higher than the end, which comes next in the circle. The end of the water tube is such that the water tends to enter from its highest point, and it leaves the system from its lowest point. To achieve this, the system uses the support of lumber for the pipes. These lumber supports also ensure that the pipes stay high above the reservoir for gravity to do its work.

Step 2: Materials required

• 66" of 4-inch PVC pipes. If you don't have any PVC pipes handy, you can also use plastic gutters.

• You will need an assortment of lumber. Visit the cull wood section at a hardware store, which includes the scraps from pre-cut wood. Choose four pieces of lumber, which are roughly 43" 2 x 4", a little plywood, and one piece of lumber which is 1.5 x 7.5 x 58".

• Plastic cups: 16-oz capacity

• Screws

• Rubber adjustable end caps fitted with hose clamps: 4

• Submersible pump

• Teflon tape

• Irrigation tubing

• Opaque bucket

• Clumping cement

• Growing medium

• Hydroponics nutrients

- Plants

Note: The dimensions will work for this system as long as they are close enough to the ones specified in this section.

Step 3: Building

Once you determine the height of the reservoir, it is time to design the stands. In this model, let us work with a reservoir that is 13". So, the stands will be about 13", 14", 15", and 16" tall (a one-inch gradient in the height of stands allows for natural flow of water). Cut the PVC tube in half and attach them together with the 2 x 4s. Attach them midway to ensure that they are both at a level.

Step 4: Plumbing

Drill a hole using a spade bit drilling tool suitable to accommodate the tubing in each of the end caps. Depending upon the water level, drill the hole at the appropriate height accordingly. Ensure that the water level is adequate so that the bottom of the cups will stay submerged. Now, take the submersible pump, and wrap one side of it with Teflon tape and use clumping cement for attaching it to the tubing. The tube should be of an ideal length such that it can run from the upper tube down to the bottom of the reservoir. Push this tube through the end hole in the cap. Now, take another piece of tube that is long enough to reach from the lower tube to the reservoir. Now, it's time to attach both the end caps using tubing of ideal length to fit comfortably with both the pieces of the PVC. Once you have built this setup, it is time to test it. If you notice any leaks, you can always use clumping cement to seal them around the tubes.

Step 5: Drilling

Depending upon the plants you want to grow, the spacing of the holes will differ. If you want to place at least six plants, the spacing between each hole must be about 8 to 9 inches. Use a 3" drill bit and cut a skewer to 3". Take this and place it in the plastic cups to see where it would fit. Now, hold this cup against the PVC and see where it would fit in its structure. Once you have drilled the holes in these areas, it is time to move on to the next step.

Step 6: Assembling

Now, it is time to bring all the previous parts together and approach the final setup. It is time to drill three holes into the lid of the bucket. One hole will accommodate the intake tube, the other for the output tube, and the final one for the power cord. By doing this, you can keep the lid on the bucket to prevent the growth of algae.

Step 7: Use plastic cups

Since you are thinking about growing six plants, take six plastic cups and drill plenty of holes in the bottom and along the edges of the plastic cup. The cups can be used for measuring out clay balls or any other growing media you want to use and place them in a bucket. Before you place the media in the cups, ensure that it has been thoroughly cleaned and rinsed. The cups must be placed in the PVC tubes that you cut out in the previous step. Make any adjustments as required to ensure the cups fit comfortably in the PVC pipes.

Step 8: Planting

Before you start planting, gently rinse the roots so that there are no traces of soil left. Once clean, surround them with the growing medium in the cups. Use a sufficient growing medium so that the cups stay upright.

Step 9: Add nutrients

Mix all the nutrients as required or follow the instructions on the premix labels. Once the nutrient solution is ready, add it to the bucket, which acts as the reservoir. Turn on the pump, and the NFT hydroponic system is ready.

The ideal plants for the NFT technique include cucumbers, spinach, kale, tomatoes, lettuce, peppers, edible flowers, and all herbs.

Chapter 6

How To Start Hydroponic Garden Step By Step

I f you do not have hundreds or thousands of dollars to spend on a growing system from the store, you can easily make your system at home. This part will teach you to build a drip-style hydroponic growing system. This particular system can be built for $60-$100, depending on where you buy your materials from.

Materials

You will need:

- 4- Five-gallon buckets

- 4 Bulkhead fittings (thread nuts)

- Submersible fountain pump

- Furnace filter

- Black (or blue) vinyl tubing for the fill and drain lines

- "T" Connectors that will fit your vinyl tubing

- 18 to 30-gallon storage tote (this will be your reservoir- bigger is better!)

- Rocks (Rinse, soak for an hour in 1-part bleach to 10 parts water and then rinse again)

48

- Growing medium (such as clay balls, Perlite, or Coconut Coir)

- Spray paint- 2 cans black and 2 cans white

- 15 Amp Timer

Other Supplies

The other things that you will need include:

- Hydroponic growth nutrients (you can make your blend if you know what you are doing)

- pH testing kit

- pH adjusters to raise or lower the pH after testing

- Rotary tool, hot metal, or something else to cut/burn/burr holes into the plastic bucket (make sure you can get the edges smooth)

- Electrical tape

- Heat source (lighter)

- Paper clip

Instructions

Before building your drip hydroponic system, you need to consider where you will be placing it. It will determine if you need more materials, such as a grow light, plastic, or bench to set your system on. The plants will grow up from the top of the open bucket, but you also have to have a drainage system at the bottom of the bucket for excess nutrients. The buckets cannot sit on the ground of a greenhouse, backyard, or other areas. Your plants are also going to need sunlight to grow, since hydroponics still require photosynthesis for the plants to be healthy and bear fruit or vegetables.

If you have a small budget, you may consider using a patio table you already have or buying 2x4s to build a bench to raise your buckets off of the ground.

1. Begin by tracing a hole in the bottom of the bucket, using the nut from the bulkhead fittings as your guidance. Do this for all buckets. The hole will be for the bulkhead fitting. Make sure this is close to the edge of the bucket, so that the system will still be stable if you stick it on a flat surface, such as the edge of a patio table. Be very cautious that the holes are not too big- otherwise your system may leak.

a. Use a drill, with the appropriate sized bit. This will help you get the round shape for the bulkhead fitting, while also keeping the edge smooth. A smooth edge is essential to ensure the fitting will line up and create a tight seal.

b. You should have an O-ring or rubber ring on the inside of the bucket to create a non-leaking seal. Some fittings may have this on the other side, right under the nut.

2. You are going to put the bulkhead fittings into the hole you have created. The fitting should be placed inside the bucket, with the longer end going through the hole to the outside. The nut will go on the outside to hold the bulkhead in place. The most extended portion of the fitting will have a tub fit over it, which is why the long side will go through the

bottom of the bucket to the outside, and then have the nut fit over it to keep it in place. Use a wrench to tighten the nut to prevent water from leaking.

a. An extra step can be to use a sealant, such as caulking around the bulkhead fitting and nut. Caulking on the outside of the fitting will not contaminate the nutrient solution, but it will prevent leaks.

b. Wait to attach the tubing to the nut.

3. You need to protect the buckets from heat and light to prevent damage to the roots and discourage the growth of algae and mold. Begin by putting electrical tape all around the bulkhead fitting- you do not want any paint to get on it! This is necessary even if you have caulked around the fitting. Make sure to cover the entire fitting, not just around the nut, since you will use spray paint. If you did caulk around the fitting wait until it is dry, it usually takes 8 hours.

4. Turn the bucket upside down on a tarp or plastic. Start spray painting several coats of black paint. You will want to do this until you cannot see any light coming through the bucket. You also need to wait for each coat of black paint to dry, before you begin the next layer. Spray paint will dry quickly; especially, in the sun. Touch the paint to check if it is dry. If it feels tacky, wait a few more minutes before spraying the next layer.

5. After the black paint is completely dry, spray a few layers of white paint over the top. Again, wait for each layer of paint to dry, before

spraying a new layer. Since black attracts heat, using white paint will help stop heat from damaging the roots.

6. While you are doing this, you should also paint the tote you are using for the reservoir. Start with a black coat and wait until it is scorched and light-proof, before adding the white layer.

7. Now that the bucket is prepared, it is time to install the filter. You will need to remove the filter part from the furnace filter. This needs to be placed across the area where the thread nuts are located. Its purpose is to keep the organic material out of the tubing, while still allowing the excess nutrient solution to drip down. Consider a vegetable container like a lettuce keeper for your fridge. There is a plastic insert in correct produce containers to ensure the product is kept from sitting in water that may be dripping off the clean vegetables. The filter will separate the rocks and growing material from the bulkhead fittings and drainage tubing.

8. You are going to lay down your rocks and your growing medium. First, lay a couple of inches of rocks at the bottom of the bucket. These will weigh down the filter, as well as keep the bucket bottom-heavy so that it is less likely to tip over, if you will keep your system outside in the wind.

9. Fill the bucket with the growing medium (fill until it is a few inches from the top of the bucket). This is the perlite, clay balls, or coconut coir. The growing medium is what will help keep the roots in place and allow the plant to grow in an upwards position, rather than falling out of the buckets.

10. Now, it is time to make the watering lines. Begin by taking tubing and making an "O". Fasten this to either end of a T-connector. Both ends of the tubing will go into the T connector to create a complete circle. The T connector will be parallel with the tubing, while the small part of the connector is still available for the incoming water line.

11. Heat the end of a paper clip and use it to make small holes in the circle tubing. Place this around your bucket. Do this for each of the 4 buckets. The holes are to allow the water nutrient solution to come out of the tubing and sink into the roots of your plants.

12. Run piping from the T-connector to your reservoir. The tube will be connected to a pump, which pumps the nutrient solution and water through the piping and into the growing medium, where the plant will absorb it.

a. The backup solution will be filtered to remove any plant matter or growing material and then drip down into a reservoir to be used again.

b. Make sure there is only one mainline going into the pump. The water pump will have an outgoing connector that your tubing will fit over. There is no need for a T-connector at the water pump.

13. Run a tube from the bulkhead fittings into the reservoir. The reservoir needs to be 6 inches from the bottom of your buckets, thus you need to measure the tube accordingly.

14. Setting up the reservoir is also needed. Painting it and getting the tubes the right length to run from the pump to the T-connector and from the bulkhead fittings to the reservoir is just a part of the reservoir

system. The filter in the bottom of the buckets is meant to catch most of the medium, so it will not go through the tubing; however, you may elect to add a filter system in the reservoir. You can divide your reservoir into two parts, where the nutrient water is kept separate from the drainage water, until it passes through a filter to clean it. You also need to have a lid for the reservoir, but access to it, so you can check the pH of the water.

15. Connect a digital timer to the pump.

If you are growing outside, you will also want to take the necessary precautions to protect your timer and electrical cords from getting wet. The first thing to do is buy all outdoor equipment, including an outdoor timer such as those made for sprinkler systems. They are designed to get wet versus indoor systems. Also, you may need lights to protect your plants from cooler temperatures depending on where you live.

Greenhouses and indoor plant rooms may also need to grow lights or plant lights to ensure they are receiving the proper sunlight and warmth. If you live in a place with four seasons or long winters, it will be necessary to have an indoor space for most fruits and vegetables.

Chapter 7

Better Materials

A ton of plants can be packed into the little space with hydroponic gardens. The plants do not need too much space, and they appear to grow more quickly when you put nutrients into the plants instead of putting them on the soil and making them search for their food. How much room you have, the type of system you want and how much you want to spend on your hydroponic garden.

The most crucial part of a water system would be the nutrient solution utilized.

Water nutrient alternatives are readily obtainable from both gardening and nursery centers. They include a combination of vitamins like potassium, phosphorus, magnesium, calcium and assorted minerals. Different nutrient reactions are utilized based on the sort of plant you attempt to grow, the machine you use as well as the press, if any, which you utilize. As we've observed, hydroponics could be performed without or utilizing the media.

In scenarios in which a broker is employed, there are lots of alternatives available, each using its blessings and pitfalls. Rockwool is among the most popular tools used in water gardening because it's low in cost and supplies smooth drainage. While dirt, sand and marbles are moderately priced and easy to acquire, they are thick. They don't offer the same level of water motion as perlite and vermiculite, which might be more significant but also more successful. Another essential problem in jelqing is the usage of lighting.

However, plants need moderate to do photosynthesis. In regions where natural lighting isn't always accessible or plentiful, HID lighting is utilized instead. There are significant kinds of lighting used in gardening, every one of which offers significant light components on the spectrum. High-pressure sodium light fittings (HPS) are similar to the abandonment of this spectrum. They are utilized for the result of flowering crops. Eventually, any thriving water system has to be tracked so that pH phases are controlled. It has to be held within a predetermined range, based upon the plant and moderate utilized.

The value could be quantified using a PH workout kit accessible at any gardening center. All you will need to prepare a normal hydroponics system

Are you excited about what you have read up to now about gardening? Here, we'll evaluate the advantages and disadvantages of this exceptional types of hydroponics instruments, and we are going to discuss the kinds of flowers which may be developed locally when utilizing these systems. When designing a regional hydroponics system, it's typically suggested to use an intermediary. Though the back apparatus is quite cheap and simple to use, it's tough to adapt over time, and so may produce awful results.

There's a challenge about if crops possess the suitable equilibrium of nourishment, also if they aren't, it can be tough to alter nourishment with circulation. Any horticultural centre, and in actuality, the majority of conventional nurseries have all of the tools required to set up a nearby device.To begin constructing a deflection and wandering equipment, you have first to get the necessary materials.

The standard machine requires:

- Container for tank

- Seeds

- Support framework for surrounding stairs

- Water pump capable of pumping at least 500 liters per hour

- Drainage pipes

- Nutrient

- 24-hour timer

- Vegetable packing containers

- Grow Tray to hold the flowers and water / nutrient solution

Caution: In case you generally employ a few of the stuff you currently have, this apparatus can be installed for USD 50. To produce your very own tidal system, fasten the seeds or pieces from the plant packaging containers, then settle them with the chosen medium, place the containers in a plastic tray and then mend them auxiliary.

Fill the tank with 3 tsp of dilute nutrient solution within 36 gallons of water. Put the tubing in a manner that runs out of the top plate into the container, then place the faucet pump in the region. The timer should just be put, so the pump gets the top container overflow cases each day.

The simplest plants to increase in house hydroponics are salad vegetables, such as spinach and lettuce.

Tomatoes, cucumbers and peppers can also be possible, even though these tools need either a high-quality bargain from natural sunlight or the inclusion of complex lamps. In case you choose to produce plants that demand a great deal of sunlight and light that's not always easy to acquire, consider incorporating an artificial lighting system.

HPS panels include exceptional illumination to flowering fruits or plants, even with greater metal halide plates such as leafy vegetables such as spinach and lettuce. It could be tricky to come up with particular vegetation to utilize a deviation and deviation system. These include berries, berries, and onion-based blossoms, including daffodils. When these programs can be grown in hydroponics, they're painted higher in most water-based systems, together with NFT or Pilates. They therefore are better suited to large industrial applications.

There's a pleasant debate within the use of herbal markers since it pertains to hydroponics. As customers emerge as more concentrated on the roots of the diets and their effect on their wellbeing, they frequently flip to the elements categorized as herbal. The prerequisites for organic labeling differ from nation to nation, with a couple of countries that believe plants without natural pesticides and unique statuses qualified for the natural mark as entirely meaning blossoms.

In the most rigorous standards, herbs are called plants growing in the floor utilizing conventional agricultural procedures. Under those criteria, chemicals or pesticides can't be used, and plant nutrients which could be implemented are rigorously controlled. Based on requirements, some foods generated in hydroponics might be called organic, since hydroponic systems don't automatically demand the use of chemicals or pesticides. But, hydroponics requires using nutrient reactions, which normally need nutrient extraction or manufacturing, then altered to become water-soluble. This manner, water blossoms aren't normal with the most rigorous tariffs, nevertheless organic in some places and across several folks can be taken into consideration. When determining whether crops grown in water can be helpful to your requirements, carefully think about your state's requirements for organic branding.

How to Pick the Best Equipment for your Hydroponic Set Up

Depending on your level of experience, finance available and requirements, the following are some of the basic equipments you will need to set up a hydroponic system. Deciding on the most useful of electronics, according to your particular gardening requirements, is likely to make the job of excelling occasionally a great deal simpler. However, below is a breakdown of the essential hydroponics gear employed in the majority of systems.

For water heater

So to give your plants with each of the water and minerals which they must survive, you've got to get your hands on a trustworthy water-pump. The sooner is set up from the nutrient solution, whereas the latter has to be set up beyond the alternate.

In case you've obtained a small installation, then a pump that provides approximately 30 to 40 mph will have the ability to offer your plants with most of the water that they need, and will not cost much better. Ensure you also consider the rate in which water drains into your growth media when choosing a water heater that satisfies the desired amount of output.

For reservoir

The reservoir used in hydroponic techniques retains the water, which subsequently retains the nutrition to be provided to your crops. Since the elementary part of any hydroponic procedure, the reservoir retains the water that's required to keep up your plants teeming with minerals and moisture. Based on your financial plan as well to how big your operation, the reservoir might be anything from a costly business version or a very simple bucket.

To decrease the evaporation of this water saved there, that will impact the nutrient equilibrium, and be certain to be in a reservoir that communicates a lid. Additional the absolute best reservoir really should not be metallic since it may get the debut of damaging minerals into this nutrient solution, or the incidence of chemical responses which may find yourself damaging your plants.

For 24hr-timer

In nearly all hydroponic methods, except that the most straightforward forms, a timer must aid with regulations of a selection of essential functions. For example, a timer may be used to regulate watering, lighting and venting cycles.

When deciding the top timer into the body, you might have two chief alternatives, easier and more affordable analog components or maybe more expensive, more advanced electronic components. The next is effective for people seeking to make a method for developing delicate plants which need extreme precision throughout the execution of every surgery.

For grow tray

You've got to keep the ph balance of this nutrient options to have any chance of creating a healthy hydroponic garden. Though some crops might have the ability to grow cheaply in a higher or lower ph degree, it's strongly recommended that you maintain it between 6 and 6.5. Of each the hydroponic equipment mentioned above, these kits are the most economical, but among the most crucial.

Growing a hydroponic garden entails less effort compared to having a garden from the earth. However, to be successful, you sure would want the exact ideal hydroponics equipment from the start, whether you opt to choose a ready-made kit or are considering putting together your own method little by bit.

For the lighting system

To enhance the progress of your plants, you must possess the appropriate older lighting fixture. It's quite important to mention during that time that although fluorescent light could be used to increase natural light, they can't, independently, give the range of light required from plants.

Metal-halide and higher pressure sodium lights were created to emit a variety of light which reproduces the quality of light emanating from the sun. Metal halide lights are the nearest you can reach the sun. They develop a much greater percentage of blue lighting that is great for supporting vegetative development.

High-pressure gaslighting, on the other hand, make mild which covers more of the red-orange spectrum. They last more, burn fuller and have an inferior quantity of energy in contrast to their metal-halide counterparts. However, they create a narrower array of lighting.

To get the best result, I suggested that you combine both types of lighting to provide light that is as close as possible to the full range of sunlight. Additionally, you will use mild reflectors and movers to cover a wider room with less lighting.

For growing media

The soil will not possess some location in hydroponics; yet , non-toxic substances are employed in its location. The evolution of media is utilized to encourage the plant as it develops.

The ideal expansion medium should be streamlined enough to anchor the plant but not too far that it disrupts the flow of air together with the nutrient solution. The particles of this medium should be able to maintain moisture and nourishment to allow the roots to absorb the crucial degree of nourishment between flood. Finally, it has to be sterile to block the propagation of fleas, diseases, and parasites.

Chapter 8

Crops Most Suitable

A t this point, it is time to start considering which fruits and vegetables that you should grow in your system. Ultimately, many can work very well in your system. Still, we are going to address just two fruits, just two vegetables, and just two herbs that you will be able to grow in your garden. While there are several options for you, and you can ultimately grow just about anything in a hydroponic system, what matters more is whether or not they are simple to maintain. Some plants are going to be inherently more difficult to manage than others. However, some are good for beginners, no matter the system that they will be using.

Hydroponic Strawberries

Strawberries are perhaps the easiest of the fruits that you can grow in a hydroponic system. Even though most of the time, fruits are harder to grow than anything else due to all of the requirements that will have to be perfect at several different stages to ensure that the plant can develop and grow, strawberries are a bit of an outlier. They are surprisingly simple to grow, and all you have to remember is how you can keep them growing with ease.

These plants can be grown year-round indoors if you can keep up with the ambient temperatures and lighting requirements. They are usually guided to produce fruits based on the temperatures that you provide and the lighting, cueing to them that it is time to produce fruit. However, if you maintain those conditions, many variants of strawberries can produce indefinitely. Keep in mind that if you want to grow strawberries, you will always want to start from a cutting or a runner instead of a seed. When you start from a seed, you must wait several years for your plant to really be developed and mature enough to be ready to grow and produce fruit. However, if you make use of a runner, the plant itself is already matured. It will simply grow outward to be large enough and then very quickly begin to produce fruit without that cooldown period.

Your strawberry plants will generally require the following ranges:

- Temperature: Between 60 and 80 degrees Fahrenheit daytime and about 10 degrees lower at night

- Nutrient solution pH: 5.8-6.2

- Nutrient solution EC: 1.4-3.0 dS/cm

- Lighting: Direct light for up to 16 hours. They need 8 hours a day of rest.

Hydroponic Tomatoes

Hydroponic tomatoes are also incredibly forgiving to grow. They will grow in just about any hydroponic setup that you can make, and assuming that you can keep your plants supported properly to allow them to grow without collapsing on themselves, your hydroponic tomatoes should be properly able to grow no matter what. These also will grow readily in most systems as well. To grow your own hydroponic tomatoes, all you have to do is make sure that you provide your plants with everything that you need, and you will see that even you can plant them indoors and have them repeatedly reproducing for you. You will get fruit year-round if you are careful about how you grow your system. Please note that tomatoes, in particular, are very dependent upon high levels of nitrogen. You need to ensure that you have a healthy load of nitrogen to ensure that your plants will grow. To grow your tomatoes, you will want to keep the following parameters:

- Temperature: 58-79 degrees Fahrenheit

- Nutrient solution pH: 5.5-6.5

- Nutrient solution EC: 2.0-5.0

- Lighting: At least 8 hours of sunlight per day

Hydroponic Cucumbers

Cucumbers are very dependent upon water—and considering just how juicy they are, there is no surprise there. If you want to grow cucumbers in your hydroponic garden, your biggest hurdle to get over will almost always be the amount of support that you can give them. Your cucumbers are very demanding for nutrients, and they are also heavily dependent upon water. So, you will need to make sure that you are providing ample water and nutrient solution. If you can remember that, your cucumbers should grow well. Generally speaking, cucumbers are great when it comes to hydroponic gardening—they love the amount of water that they can get, and they will grow with ease in most setups. To grow your hydroponic cucumbers, you will need to remember that they will need support. If you cannot give them that support, you will struggle to keep them growing. The easiest way that you can help support them is with trellis wire and training.

- Temperature: 75-85 degrees Fahrenheit

- Nutrient solution pH: 5.5

- Nutrient solution EC: 2-3

- Lighting: High light during the day for at least 14 hours

Hydroponic Spinach

Spinach, like most other leafy greens, thrive in hydroponic systems. They love the constant access to the solution that is there for them, and if you can maintain their temperatures and lighting requirements, they will grow very well. However, you must keep in mind that these plants will bolt readily if they are kept in warmer temperatures. This is a huge problem—if you allow your plants to bolt, they will flower to create seeds, and when that happens, the spinach becomes bitter and tastes bad. When that happens, you will not want to eat it.

- Temperature: No higher than 75 degrees Fahrenheit, but preferably between 60 and 70 degrees Fahrenheit.

- Nutrient solution pH: 6.0-7.0

- Nutrient solution EC: 1.8-2.3

- Lighting: These plants prefer lower levels of lighting. In particular, they make use of 12 hours of lower-level lighting.

Sunlight, especially in summer months, is too much for them. They will prefer some degree of shade. You will want to use lights that are on the bluer end of the spectrum.

Hydroponic Parsley

You may not think of growing your won parsley, but it is actually a very handy garnish to have on hand. It is flavorful and tasty, and can also be used widely in just about any cuisine. It is also very hardy—it has wide ranges for temperature, pH, and EC, and because of that and the fact that you do not want it to flower, you are able to grow large amounts of it with ease. Even better, the more you crop down, the more will grow back, meaning you can grow a plant and have it regrow for future harvests. Parsley would lend itself well to a small countertop growing setup if you had one, and it is incredibly flexible. This means that you will be able to have it growing in your home with little space requirement, and usually, the first harvest only takes about 2 to 2.5 months after beginning to grow it. If you want to try your hand at parsley, you will need to keep the following conditions:

- Temperature: 60-75 degrees Fahrenheit

- Nutrient solution pH: 5.5-6.0

- Nutrient solution EC: 0.8-1.8

- Lighting: Parsley usually loves full light. It can usually do well under fluorescent lights, but it will prefer higher spectrum light.

Hydroponic Basil

Basil is another plant that can really thrive if you were to grow it in a hydroponic setting. You could grow it on your countertop if you wanted just a small supply of it, or you could grow an entire system's worth of basil if you and your family are particularly partial to pesto or other foods that heavily feature basil. Thanks to the fact that it is not necessary to allow basil to flower, you can really make use of the fact that it is quite simple to grow indoors. Especially if you find that you will use basil regularly, growing it yourself will be far more economical in the long run for an extended period of time. One well-cared-for plant will provide you with roughly ½ a cup of basil weekly, though you can grow more very easily as well, especially in a hydroponic setup where you will naturally be boosting your production just by virtue of the way that the system will grow. When it comes to growing basil, you must keep in mind that it is sensitive to cold—this means that if you want to plant it and encourage it to keep growing, you will really need to ensure that you do not allow it to get too cold; otherwise, you risk the plant failing to thrive.

- Temperature: 70-85 degrees Fahrenheit

- Nutrient solution pH: 6.2-6.8

- Nutrient Solution EC: 1.6-2.2

- Lighting: This plant prefers full lighting—it will require at least 14-18 hours per day of full light.

Chapter 9

How To Set Up Your Own Hydroponics Garden

Over the years, the use of hydroponics has been taken into consideration and also, adopted by a good number of people that seek to upgrade their farming. Hydroponics is all about setting up a means to grow plants in a modern liquid solution, rather than having the plants grow up in the soil. People often go for this solution when they are determined to get the best out of the plants. There are plant diseases that go with the soil, and the cause of the disease may be an attack from insects and other plant predators. In a situation where one uses the hydroponics system, such things do not exist, since there is no soil for the insects and other predators to attack. Going for this system saves you from having to weed from time to time; it also saves you water too. When compared to the plants raised on the soil, the plants raised on the hydroponics system outgrows their rivalry by 25% and in the rate of production, they do better than their opponent by 30%. This is why most people do go for this hydroponics system because they are sure to give you more than you ever expect so long as you give them what they need and at the right quantity. Making or growing a garden with the use of the hydroponics system is a very good and wonderful idea. It will be a beauty to behold, following this course. For one to set a hydroponics garden, there are some things that you need to take into consideration and work towards. Below are the leading ways and factors that you should work with as you set up this system of raising good and great plants without the use of soil.

1. The Right Side of the garden

A hydroponics garden can be an exterior or interior one, that is one of the reasons people do go for it. The hydroponics system should be located on a leveled ground so that the water and the nutrients will be on a level to mix up well and give the plants what they need. If you want to have it outside your apartment, then you should set up barriers for elements that will bring harm to them. The elements can be in the form of wind, flood, overheating from the sun which will cause the water in the nutrients to evaporate, pests and others. One is advised not to leave the hydroponics system outside when the temperature is cold. Have the hydroponics system inside with enough lighting during the winter period or whenever the climate is not safe for the plants. Whichever place you choose to have the garden, make sure that the temperature there is the best for the plants. Such a place should have its temperature ranging from sixty-five to eighty degrees (65-80°). While setting up the garden, one is also advised to have it in a small size, if one is starting it up for the first time. It should not take too much space at first so that it can be of good management. As time goes on, the person can now expand the garden and grow as many plants, crops and flowers in the quantity he or she desires. The location for the garden should have enough space depending on the number of plants you want to have there. The space for the garden should be equipped with enough lights so that the plants can grow as desired. For a hydroponics garden, you can go to an indoor greenhouse. This is what people that are starting the hydroponics system new usually go for. As you start with a small unit of the garden, both in size of the area and the same of the plants, you begin to experience what it feels like to have an indoor garden of your own and then, prepare yourself for the bigger phase. Gardens are not just meant to grow plants and flowers of different species, they are also there for aesthetic reasons, the beauty they give, the serene and glorious environment that goes with them too. This is why you need to grow your hydroponics garden in that part of your house that delights you, which should also be good and well-kept for the growth of the plants and flowers. Remember to have the light factor and the level of the ground or base area in mind as you do this. You can go for a humidifier if that part of the house is dry. Just make sure the hydroponics system is kept in a plant-friendly environment and watch the plants grow as you like it. The part of the house you should choose for the garden should also be where children will not get close to the system, so as to prevent damage or harm of any kind. The indoor greenhouse style is usually employed by the people that are starting the hydroponics system of gardening newly while the closet hydroponics system is usually meant for the people that have a little space for the garden. Since it is a hydroponics garden, you do not need soil to have your plants grow, you just need your plants, flowers, nutrients, and water set in place in your closet; that is if you choose to go for the closet hydroponics style. If your house or apartment is not a big one, you can make use of your closet for gardening. With the light factor in place, an enclosed box, proper ventilation, and other necessary factors, one can make a good hydroponics garden. The gardening will not be an easy one since space for the plants to grow in is not a big one. The gardener will have to pay close attention to the plants; the light factor and climate conditions should also be taken seriously at every interval to prevent loss. The ventilation should also be looked into from time to time. The gardener should check the plants regularly. If you choose to go for an exterior hydroponics system, you can employ the patio garden style. This style is a very good one due to the environment, the sun, the atmosphere; but do not forget that it is not suitable for the plants during the winter season. You can also situate your hydroponics garden in a greenhouse. A greenhouse provides the plants with the right and nice environment that is good for gardening. The temperature, ventilation, and lighting are nice when they are planned out very well. The greenhouse can come in different styles; there is the attached-single slope, the barn style, A-frame style, Gothic arch, and others, depending on how it was built and the design or designs given to the house. Whichever place you may choose to locate the hydroponics garden, make sure there is enough lighting, ventilation, space, a leveled ground and other necessary factors planned for there. Remember that a hydroponics garden can be placed inside and outside the house so long as the conditions necessary for keeping them where you have chosen are met.

2. Laying out the hydroponics structure

There are too many structures that one can use to set up the hydroponics garden. The structures all depend on the location of the garden, the climatic conditions, the light factor, the size of the plants

75

and structure, the design you choose for the structure and so many other factors. The structures resemble the wick system. This wick system has been in use in the hydroponics world for a good number of years, if not ages. Here, the use of water pumps is not necessary since the wick passes the water itself and the nutrients down the root of the plants. You are advised to get the equipment you will use for the wicks hydroponics growing system ready so that you can start up the garden without wasting time. Use a black container to prepare a reservoir solution for the growth system. Make room for the checking of the level of the nutrient solution. Using the size of the container reservoir which you already have, cut out and prepare the Styrofoam to fit the reservoir solution. On the Styrofoam, use a pencil to mark out and then, cut out holes which will be for the net pots. Cut out a hole at the edge of the Styrofoam; this will be for the airline. For the hydroponics system itself, have the reservoir tank which you have in a place filled with the nutrient solution which you have prepared. Remember not to overfill or underfill it. It should be at a normal rate or level. Have the airstone inside the nutrient solution, but not before you have the airstone connected to the air pump. The Styrofoam should be in the tank, and the air tubing should go through the right hole meant for it. As for the net pots, have them filled with the proper level of the growing medium and each one of the pots should have a plant properly planted for the hydroponics growth to begin. Each one of the pots should have a wick, which should be covered by the growing medium, and the ones at the downside of the pots should be very long and not short. The holes which you have already made are the right places on which your pots should be. The downside of the pot should not be too close to the solution. At this point, all you need to do is to turn on the air pump and see the wick hydroponics growing structure which you have built by just following the instructions given. From time to time, use clean water to flush the medium so as to maintain your structure and have it in a good place. Take precautions when handling the structure, so that it will last long for you.

There is the deep water culture hydroponics system. This particular system is also called the reservoir method. Here, the hydroponics structure is very easy to build and manage; in fact, it is the easiest system out of the six major hydroponic systems. Here, the growing medium, which is found inside the mesh basket houses the plants. The medium acts as an aid to the plant since it does not pass the required nutrients to the plants. The mesh basket will now be placed in a reservoir that has a nutrient solution inside of it. The holes in the mesh basket will serve as passages for the roots of the plants, which will continually go down into the solution of nutrients as the plants grow. The airstone which is found under the reservoir should be connected to the aquarium pump, as air goes through the solution, and down to the roots of the plants. In this system, the light is very harmful to the roots of the plants, but not the same as the leaves. So, the structure should be fashioned in such a way that the walls of the reservoir will be light proof, so as to prevent light from passing to the roots and the nutrient solution. As it is with the wicks growing system, the structure and nutrients solution should be checked from time to time, so that the nutrients can be changed to prevent any case of toxicity or any issue of that kind.

Chapter 10

Choosing the Right Medium for Your Hydroponic System

The first picture that comes to everyone's minds when they think about growing plants is that they are growing in soil. But in hydroponics, we have seen an alternative, and that is – plants do not always require soil for growing. They can be grown in other types of media as well. In hydroponics, we provide the plants with a nutrient solution that is water-based, but there is still a requirement of a medium, which is also known as a substrate. The medium that you need will also vary with the type of hydroponics system you are choosing but, in this chapter,, you will learn about some of the most common choices when it comes to growing media.

Now, you must be wondering why we need the medium in the first place. Well, for starters, the medium helps in giving stability to the plant by supporting its weight. Secondly, the root system of the plant takes in oxygen and moisture from the medium. So, the medium is actually responsible for helping the plants get exposure to the nutrients it needs.

But do you know why it is better to grow your plants in a soil-less media? Diseases and pests are something that occurs in a greater frequency when you grow your plants in the soil, but with a hydroponics system, this risk reduces. Also, you do not always have soil in all places like your terrace or your patio. Sometimes, there is soil, but the soil is not suitable for growing anything, and in all these cases, the hydroponic system can be truly beneficial.

Another great benefit of using a medium other than soil is that you do not have to worry about weeds. You also get to control the entire environment in which the plants are growing. When plants grow in soil, they literally have to do all the work in searching for the nutrients, but when you are growing them in the media, all the nutrients are already present since you are giving the nutrient-rich solution to the media. The plant does not have to expend any energy in searching for the nutrients, and this, in turn, enables the plants to grow faster.

Forms of Growing Media

There are different forms of growing media for a hydroponic system, and here, we are going to discuss them in detail –

Grains and Pebbles

This first one is grains and pebbles, and this medium is used in those plants whose roots need space to expand and grow and also need maximum aeration. There are different types of media in this category and some of them are also responsible for providing moisture. There are others whose main function is to facilitate drainage. Some common examples are river rock, sand, perlite, grow stones, vermiculite, and so on.

Foam Matrix

The next type of media that we are going to discuss is the foam media, and they are usually available in the form of cubes. They have a very solid and firm structure and have an excellent capacity for retaining moisture, and this is why they are great for transplants, cuttings, and seeds. They are available in the form of rolls and large sheets and that is why they are one of the best options when it comes to being used as a primary substrate. Some of the common examples are floral foam, oasis cubes, and rockwool.

Fibrous Organic Matter

These are somewhat a mixture of the above two forms. They have an overall fibrous appearance, but they also have individual particles. Some common examples are pine bark, coco coir, and pine shavings. These are not so much common as the above two varieties of mediums.

The Ultimate List of Growing Media

Now, in this list, we are going to learn about each of the growing mediums in detail –

LECA

Some of the other names that are used to describe this media are clay pebbles, clay pellets, and grow rock. This substrate is made in such a way that the clay pellets become highly lightweight and porous. For this, the pellets are fired in a particular manner, which makes them take the shape of popcorn. Even though they are light in weight, they have enough mass to provide support to the plants.

This medium is completely pH neutral and sterile. No matter how much time has passed, they will not shrink or become compact. You can simply re-sterilize and clean the pellets so that they can be reused again. But if you think of it on a large scale then the process can become extensive and time-consuming.

Perlite

This is a medium that is a known name to many traditional gardeners. For years, perlite has been used in soil mixes to provide sufficient aeration. This porous material is extremely lightweight and is manufactured from volcanic glass by air-puffing them. The porousness of the media makes it one of the best when it comes to retaining oxygen. But in certain types of hydroponic systems, the weight of perlite becomes a disadvantage. This is especially true in the case of a system where water will come in direct contact and cause the perlite granules to shift. Ultimately, they get washed away. That is why this growing media is not used alone but is mixed with others like vermiculite, or coco coir.

Now, there are different types of perlite, and people often get confused as to which one they should use. If you want a greater drainage capability, then you should consider getting the coarse perlite because they also have a greater air porosity. They make sure that the roots have proper breathability. If you are in for some crops that grow for a long-term, then perlite is going to be the best media for the job because there is literally no cation exchange involved. But at the same, you should also keep a check on whether the plant has moisture deficiencies or not because perlite does not hold any amount of water.

Growstones

In some ways, LECA and growstones are similar. Growstones are also lightweight and have a porous nature, and they are made from recycled glass. They are reusable too. At first, a powdery form is made from glass bottles that are collected from different landfills. Then that powder is melted, and calcium carbonate is mixed in that mixture. Once the mixture starts bubbling, it is cooled completely. After that, it is broken to form the growstones. But there is one disadvantage to these and that is, if you are going to change the media, you should be careful as the growstones tend to grip the roots of the plants strongly. This causes a lot of root damage. So, if you are using growstones, it is better to use them as a permanent bed.

Vermiculite

Perlite and vermiculite are very similar to one another. It is also a type of expanded mineral. But the cation-exchange capacity of vermiculite is greater than that of perlite. That is why this medium is able to keep the unused minerals within it so that if the plants require those minerals later, the medium released it. The water retention capability of vermiculite is really good.

SAP

SAP stands for Super Absorbent Polymer, and some alternative names for this material are hydrogels, water beads, water crystal gel, and so on. As compared to its mass, SAP has the capability of absorbing a huge quantity of liquid. This particular media is not only meant for hydroponic systems but has a lot of industrial uses as well. One such use of this media is that it is used in flood control systems and also in cold therapy packs.

The beads of SAP are reusable and quite inexpensive. There are several sizes, and you can choose the one that suits your hydroponic system the best. For better root growth and aeration, go for the granules that are of a larger size. If you want the roots of the plants to get a better supply of oxygen, then you can use SAP after mixing with some other medium.

Sand

One of the cheapest media you will get is sand. It is available in abundance, and if you are just starting out, then sand can be great. But there are some things that you have to keep in mind and that is – sand can be quite heavy, has an extremely low capacity of water retention, and has to be sterilized frequently.

Rockwool

This particular hydroponic medium has been in the market for several decades. Long and thin fibers are made by melting rock (the process is very similar to that of fiberglass). Then, solid cubes are made of different sizes by pressing those fibers into these shapes. Although the media has some serious downsides, the benefits are also endless. One of the main downsides is that there is a problem of disposal, especially because the fibers are made from rocks, and so they are probably going to last for a long time. Also, they need a lot of soaking and have a high pH level. The compressing process creates a lot of dust which can be harmful to health. But there is a way in which you can prevent the dust, that is –

soak the cubes in water as soon as you take them out, and in this way, you do not have to inhale the dust.

Now, let us talk about the benefits. Rockwool can retain air and water, and it is sterile too. It also helps to keep the plant stable because of its solid structure.

Chapter 11

Starting Seeds and Cloning

The best way to start seeds is to use a seed starter cube. A cube the size of one and a half inch will fit perfectly in a two-inch net pot. These small cubes are capable of holding water while air can reach the roots, which is the most important while germinating seeds.

First, you need to soak your grow cubes in chlorine or chloramine free water with a pH of 5.5. Water from your tap will be around 7-8 pH. You most likely need to use a pH down solution.

Getting the chlorine out of your tap water is quite easy. Let it sit for one day for the chlorine to evaporate. If you want it to evaporate faster, you can use an air stone to air the chlorine out much quicker.

If your water company uses chloramine, you need a reverse osmosis filter to remove the chloramine. Note that not every reverse osmosis filter can remove chloramine. Chloramine can't be aired out and needs to be filtered. If you do not have a reverse osmosis filter available, you can use one thousand mg (one gram) of vitamin C (ascorbic acid) per forty gallons (one hundred and fifty liters) of water.

Use a tray to soak the cubes, pour the water on top, and let it sit for a few minutes. Once most of the water is absorbed, you need to drain the rest of the water. Do not squeeze the cubes. This will remove air pockets inside the cubes.

The next step is dropping your seeds into the holes. This can be a big task if you need to do a lot of seeds. Commercial growers use pelleted seeds and a vacuum seeder to speed this process up. Pelleted seed is a seed that is wrapped in clay. it is bigger, thus easier to handle.

You could also use a toothpick and dip the tip in some water. This will make the seed stick to the toothpick, as shown in the following image.

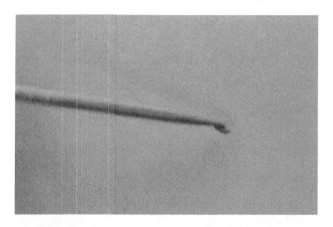

Using a wet toothpick to pick up seeds

Placing the seed into the seed starter cube

If the holes of the grow media are preventing you from dropping the seed in, use a pen or a toothpick to open the hole back up.

You can use more than one seed per hole if the germination rate is bad. I always use two seeds per hole. When both seeds germinate, I keep the best one and use scissors to remove the bad one.

Next, place your humidity dome on top of the tray to keep the seed starter cubes moist. Generally, the seeds don't need water until they have germinated. If you notice that your seed starter cubes are drying out, you can pour some more water in the tray. Do not forget to drain the rest of the water.

Once the seeds start showing its first two leaves, you need to put it under a light source. This will provide the plant with the energy they need to grow. If you experience that the stems are growing long (stretching). It means that your plant is reaching for the light. Increase the light on the seedlings to avoid this stretching. Do not use red lights on seedlings. White fluorescents that are 6500K are perfect.

After ten days, you can transplant them to your system. If you are growing in a greenhouse, it can take fifteen days in winter.

Seedling Stage

Once your seedling has become strong enough, they can be transplanted into the hydroponic growing media. In general, once your seedling has produced a couple of true leaves, it is ready to be transplanted. The true leaves will not be the first leaves the plant forms. The first one to three leaves is known as cotyledons. The true leaves come after those and are often larger and darker.

When you transplant, you want to make sure that the growing media is supporting the plant so that it sits upright and is stable. The roots need to be completely covered so that they will be in the nutrient mixture.

Vegetative Stage

Once your plant is in your hydroponic system, you have to make sure that it has everything it needs. That means you need to check the pH and everything of your nutrient solution to make sure it is getting the nutrients and oxygen that it needs. Also, make sure that you are keeping up with the correct lighting schedule for your plant. It is the first few weeks of life in your system that are the most important. They can make or break your plant.

There is something that you have to keep an eye on during your plant's entire life, and those are pests. You may be wondering how hydroponic plants that are grown inside could face pests, but they do. If you do not prepare yourself for them, an infestation could undo all of your hard work. Let's take some time to discuss pests and how to prevent them from infesting your hydroponic plants.

Flowering Stage

Some plants will require pollination for them to produce their vegetable. Some plants self-pollinate, and you will not have to worry about pollination. Something that people may take for granted when growing plants is when they are grown outside in a regular garden is that bees or butterflies and other animals naturally pollinate your plants.

When the plant is brought inside into a hydroponic system, you no longer have natural pollinators working for you. To some degree, you may have some natural pollination with the movement of air, vibration, or shaking when plants are pruned or trained, but you cannot count on that.

How to pollinate plants will all depend on the plant itself. The majority of fruit-bearing species will require some type of pollination, with the one exception being commercial hydroponic cucumbers, which exhibit a parthenocarpy fruit set. Eggplants, peppers, strawberries, melons, and tomatoes will all benefit from some pollination assistance.

Luckily, this will not involve precise work, at least for the most part. The most common type of pollination is hand pollination. It is very efficient, cheap, and flexible. The main thing you have to think about is timing. Pollen on the flower is only viable for a very short period, and flowers tend to open quickly under the right growing conditions, so you have a very small window to do this.

The rapid but gentle movement of the flower will release the pollen from the flower anthers. It will look like a cloud of yellow dust. Once it has been released, the pollen will fall onto the stigma and will start to germinate. The pollen tube will grow into the style, and the fertilization process will occur after a few hours. Fertilization of your plant's flower will result in the creation of seeds. In plants like peppers and tomatoes, the number of seeds and the growth hormone that it releases will determine how big the fruit gets.

When it comes to fruiting crops like melons, hand pollination can become more complex. These plants grow male and female flowers and the pollen from the male flower has to be transferred to the female flower. You will have to pluck the male flowers from the plant, strip back the petals, and their stamen has to be wiped over the stigma of the female flowers.

Male flowers will start being produced weeks before the plant starts producing female flowers, so you will have to be patient. You can differentiate the two because the female flower will have a small, green fruitlet, or egg, at the base of the flower. This is perfectly normal and helps prevent the plant from producing more fruit than it will be able to support. This is why vining plants, like melons and pumpkins, will produce a lot of flowers but not nearly as many fruits.

Lastly, you can use artificial wind pollination on some plants. Crops like strawberries, which are mainly self-pollinating, benefit from the assistance of the artificial wind. All this will involve is moving large air blowers over the crop rows at the height of the plant after they have started to form flowers. You can do this on small hydroponic systems with a hairdryer set to cool.

Harvest Stage and Crops

Once your plant has grown its fruit or vegetable, you get to harvest it just like you would with a regular garden. Now, there is one exception to this. If you do any research on hydroponic harvesting, you will come across harvesting hydroponic lettuce.

You have two choices when it comes to harvesting lettuce. One is with roots, and the other is without roots. To harvest with roots, get containers for the lettuce ready and wash your hands. Mist your plants with some freshwater before and during the harvesting. Gently hold onto the lettuce and lift it out of the hydroponic solution. Let the solution drain away and then place the lettuce in the container. Lettuce the roots attached will last you for two to three weeks.

Chapter 12

Crop Health

C rop health is of foremost significance to ranchers; along these lines, cautious and steady checking of crop health is a flat out must. An ongoing report on espresso yield misfortunes from 2013 to 2015 uncovered that vermin and illnesses prompted high essential (26%) and auxiliary (38%) yield misfortunes in the specialist's examined zone. This features the importance of intently focusing on such hindering elements in your crop's condition. Doing so will guarantee most extreme return and benefit for ranchers come collect time.

To take a gander at crop health observing as administered by only a couple of angles, in any case, is a genuine misstep. Or maybe, a comprehensive methodology must be embraced; at the end of the day, a bigger number of elements should be checked than just epidemic and malady.

Here are seven of the most significant crop health measurements for ranchers to screen, in light of the Sustainable Agriculture Research and Education (SARE) Program's rules.

1) Crop appearance

Maybe the most evident marker of crop health is their outward presentation. While not an across the board, secure technique for checking the present state of a specific arrangement of crops, a rancher having the correct devices and information can tell a considerable amount from just taking a gander at the condition of their plants.

Delicacy or staining in foliage as a rule focuses to chlorosis, a state where plants produce lacking chlorophyll. Current strategies for crop health observing, including new advances that use both close infrared and obvious light, permit ranchers to effectively and precisely screen chlorophyll content.

2) Crop development

Among the pointers of poor crop development are short branches, scanty stand, and the irregularity or nonattendance of new shoots. This, obviously, will definitely influence your absolute yield in a negative manner. Under perfect conditions, there ought to be vigorous development and thick, uniform sub your crops.

3) Tolerance or protection from stress

Basically, crop pressure is an abatement in crop creation realized by outer elements. A model would be presentation to abundance light and high temperatures, which may upset photosynthesis (known as photoinhibition). Accordingly, crops will have inadequate vitality to manage organic product or develop, and may even continue enduring harm to their layers, chloroplasts, and cells. Healthy crops are pressure tolerant and can without much of a stretch skip back in the wake of being presented to stressors in their condition.

4) Occurrences of nuisances and additionally illnesses

A marker that your crops are incredibly vulnerable to nuisances and illnesses would be if over half of the populace winds up getting harmed by said factors. Under the correct conditions, under 20% of your crops would be contrarily influenced by any attack of nuisances or spread of ailment, permitting them to recover and increment in number again handily.

Building crop obstruction against unsafe creepy crawlies and ailments should be possible in various manners, including improving crop decent variety, crop pivot, utilizing natural pesticides, for example, Himalayan salt shower and eucalyptus oil, and even hereditary research and improvement.

5) Weed rivalry and weight

Aside from creepy crawlies and plant ailments, weeds can likewise spell fate for your crops, whenever left unchecked. If your ranch becomes overpopulated with weeds that will take the supplements from your crops, you will positively see that your crops are consistently decreasing. Healthy crops, then again, would inevitably overpower the weed populace and recover strength over your field.

6) Genetic assorted variety

To have just a single predominant assortment of crop in your homestead is commensurate to placing your eggs in a solitary crate. For example, you ought to consider the significance of having various infection safe crop assortments on your ranch. Try not to fall prey to the enticement of supplanting them altogether with a solitary, higher-yielding sort.

It is basic to buil crop opposition against unsafe creepy crawlies and maladies

7) Plant decent variety and populace

In a perfect setting, there ought to be multiple types of plants in your field. Tallying the genuine number of trees or plants over your homestead, just as the normally happening vegetation on all sides of the zone, can likewise give you a superior point of view on your ranch's general crop health.

A hydroponic harvest alludes to the yield that is developed (delivered) in a hydroponic nursery. The term hydroponic yields can likewise allude to a plant that can be developed effectively utilizing hydroponics. Lettuce, tomatoes, peppers, beans, and cucumbers, for instance, are on the whole reasonable hydroponic yields.

Hydroponic yields for the most part incorporate nourishment crops as opposed to fancy harvests, for example, blossoms, yet many sharp hydroponic producers are beginning to develop blossoms notwithstanding eatable harvests.

Hydroponic planting resembles no other sort of cultivating. Right now, are developed with no dirt and are continually taken care of a supplement arrangement that is siphoned from a tank (store) and is frequently consistently reused all through the framework.

Maximum Yield clarifies Hydroponic Crops

Plants developed in a hydroponic nursery are normally developed in plate that are somewhat calculated so as to permit the supplement answer for stream back to the holding tank through gravity. The plants, which are developed without soil, are moored in the plate with an idle material, for example, earth, sand, rockwool, or coco coir.

Hydroponic harvests must be firmly observed and pruned explicitly to create exceptional returns. Hydroponic harvest yields can be up to multiple times higher than customarily developed plants, when things like vertical frameworks and controlled condition horticulture are considered.

Hydroponic yields are those assortments that don't require a ton of room and don't set aside an excessively long effort to develop. Lettuce, tomatoes, and beans are largely astounding hydroponic harvests, as are squash, melons, cucumbers, and leeks. Harvests like corn or wheat, which require a great deal of real esatate so as to deliver critical yields, are basically not viable to develop in a hydroponic nursery or framework. Carrots are likewise unsatisfactory for hydroponics since they would require profound develop beds.

Hydroponic harvest yields are cleaner and less inclined to contain contaminants or pesticides. Since hydroponic nurseries are regularly developed inside, they're not dependent upon similar poisons or bugs of an ordinary nursery or field.

Developing green produce in soil has its difficulties. On account of (moderately) little scope creation – the focal point of this specialized book, huge numbers of these difficulties are viable in nature. On the off chance that plants are at ground level they are more diligently to collect, a bother for 'pick your own' clients, and they additionally require a lot of room, expect revolution to forestall sickness develop, and high fruitfulness. Various yields require insurance systems to broaden the season, which means moving physical structures, or expanding inputs. Consistency of fertilization and steady quality (for fruiting yields) are likewise hard to guarantee.

While hydroponic developing frameworks are not an 'enchantment projectile' of reasonable nourishment creation (as they are now and again proposed to be) they offer handy points of interest which can bolster a more extensive scope of plant crops, or empower expansion into agricultural creation. The book examines the hydroponic strategies included, the prerequisites for a producer, and the yields which are most appropriate to development in these frameworks. Preventative notes are given on normal difficulties, and their restrictions are examined. Just 7% of Welsh land is arranged in the best 3 evaluations for green development, in this manner hydroponic frameworks offer a way to build the measure of plant creation to satisfy need for new produce.

Chapter 13

Tips and Tricks for Beginners

This chapter is all about giving you as many tips and tricks that you can use to help succeed at hydroponic gardening. We are all beginners at different points in time, and that is okay! But, the sooner that you learn the ins and outs of your system and how to succeed, the more likely that it is that your plants will thrive

Always know what you need ahead of time

Before you begin, make sure that you go over everything that you need. Write out the plans for your system and know exactly which equipment you will need and the purpose it will serve. This will help immensely with the planning portion of the garden and will help you ensure that you get everything that you need.

Always keep a backup of common items

It is all too common for something to happen when you least expect it or when it will cause a big problem for you. For this reason, you should make sure that you always store extra supplies on hand to ensure that your system will be better armed with the supplies that it will need. For example, keep extra tubing and light bulbs on hand.

Write up your schedule before you begin your garden

This will be your timing for when you can expect yourself to go out and do your daily, weekly, and monthly checks for your garden. You should commit before you build, so you know exactly what to expect.

Avoid light on your nutrient solution

It is way too easy to get algae in these systems—algae thrives on the nutrients that you have saturated into it. It is much better for you to simply cut out the light source entirely from the solution so you can prevent algae development.

Do not enter the room during dark periods

If your garden is set to be dark every night from 7pm to 5am, then you cannot enter the room at all during this period. You do not want any light on the plants at all while they are resting.

Always sterilize between crops

You must ensure that your tank is healthy, and the best way to do so is to make sure that your entire system is sterilized long before you add your newest crops. Any time that you are changing to a new crop, such as at a new season, you must always clean the entire thing from top to bottom. This helps prevent any cross-contamination.

Keep new plants in a 2-week quarantine

To prevent any infection, any time that you get a new plant, allow them to grow on their own for at least two weeks. This will allow them to either show signs of illness if there are any or prove that they are clean and, therefore, safe to add to your own garden. Plants can pass illnesses and diseases around very quickly, and it is better to avoid this altogether.

Avoid your garden after having been outdoors or in another garden

Along those same lines, you should try to visit your own garden after you have showered exclusively and after you have changed your clothes. You should never enter after you have been around other plants, as that ups the risk of infecting your own system, and you are supposed to be keeping your own system sanitized.

Make sure climate control is constant in your garden

You want to protect your garden as much as possible—and that means ensuring that you protect the plants and their environment. You want to make sure that the garden's environment is as consistent as possible.

Choose plants with similar parameters

If you can make sure that all of your plants have very similar requirements, you can protect your entire system from failing. You will be more likely to succeed if all of your plants want the same lighting, nutritional value, and global temperatures. They may have different ranges, but if those ranges overlap, they can usually do just fine in tandem with each other

Conclusion

Congratulations! You have made it to the end of Hydroponics. You have officially been guided through all of the fundamental information that you will need to get started on your own hydroponic journey. No matter what your budget is, what you are comfortable spending, whether you are interested in growing plants from your area or from somewhere far away from you, or whether you would like to garden throughout the winter, there is a system that will work for you, and hopefully, you have come to recognize that.

This book aimed to teach you everything that you would need to decide whether or not hydroponic gardening was for you. And, the answer is hopefully, yes! It is! This is perhaps one of the most hands-off gardening methods that you can use if you want to grow fruits and vegetables at home, or even inside the comfort of your own home. If you are able to set up even a small corner of your home or set up a small space on your windowsill, you too can begin to garden from home. No matter the budget, there are options for you. No matter how much space you have, or even how much time you have, you can make this gardening work for you.

Remember, you should always weigh heavily what your own constraints are before you get involved with any sort of gardening at all. This means that you must identify the space that you have available, consider the budget that is set for you, and recognize that ultimately, you can do this before you begin. You need to have a plan made, deciding which form of garden you would like to pursue and which plants are the best fit for you. If you can keep up with this, and you can guide yourself through the decision-making process, you should be able to succeed with ease with these systems.

From here, it is time for you to begin to decide what it is that you would like to grow. Would you love an endless supply of strawberries or basil? Do you want fresh tomatoes on demand? You can make either of those happen if you are willing to set up the necessary space for them. If you can do that, you can succeed in gardening any of these, so long as you spend the time maintaining the climate and requirements that your plants have.

This means that you can grow that big tomato bush in your apartment. You can grow strawberries for your kids to eat on demand. You can grow herbs, garlic, onions, or just about any other small plant, all from indoors, if you are willing to give it a shot, and you now know-how.

Do not forget the value of being able to eliminate soil from your gardening. Do not forget that these plants can be so much more prolific than their soil-grown peers. Do not forget that you will be able to grow more plants than ever before, using less space.

Thank you once more for picking up this book and deciding to read it. Hopefully, you feel like you have gotten all of those questions that you had floating around in your head answered, and hopefully, you feel like you can succeed with the knowledge that you now have!

Finally, if you have found that this has been a helpful introduction to gardening, please head over to Amazon to leave a review! Hearing feedback from the readers is always greatly appreciated!

Made in the USA
Las Vegas, NV
17 November 2023

81053110R00066